anythink

D0602489

NO LONGER PROPERTY OF
ANYTHINK LIBRARIES/
RANGEVIEW LIBRARY DISTRICT

Author Biographies

Beatrix Potter

Charlotte Guillain

Heinemann Library
Chicago, Illinois

www.capstonepub.com
Visit our website to find out more information about Heinemann-Raintree books.

To order:

☎ Phone 888-454-2279

💻 Visit www.capstonepub.com to browse our catalog and order online.

© 2012 Heinemann Library
an imprint of Capstone Global Library, LLC
Chicago, Illinois

All rights reserved. No part of this publication may be reproduced or transmitted in any form or by any means, electronic or mechanical, including photocopying, recording, taping, or any information storage and retrieval system, without permission in writing from the publisher.

Edited by Rebecca Rissman, Daniel Nunn, and Sian Smith
Designed by Joanna Hinton-Malivoire
Picture research by Tracy Cummins
Production by Victoria Fitzgerald
Originated by Capstone Global Library Ltd
Printed and bound in China by South China Printing Company Ltd

15 14 13 12 11
10 9 8 7 6 5 4 3 2 1

Library of Congress Cataloging-in-Publication Data
Guillain, Charlotte.
Beatrix Potter / Charlotte Guillain.
p.cm.—(Author biographies)
Includes bibliographical references and index.
ISBN 978-1-4329-5960-9 (hardback)
ISBN 978-1-4329-5966-1 (paperback)
1. Potter, Beatrix, 1866-1943—Juvenile literature.
2. Authors, English—20th century—Biography—Juvenile literature. 3. Artists—Great Britain—Biography—Juvenile literature. 4. Children's stories—Authorship—Juvenile literature. I. Title.
 PR6031.O72Z5865 2012
 823'.912—dc22   2011016063
 [B]

Acknowledgments
We would like to thank the following for permission to reproduce photographs: Alamy Images pp. 5 (© UrbanZone), 9, 18 (© The National Trust Photolibrary), 14 (© David Cheshire), 15 (© Pictorial Press Ltd), 20 (© David Taylor); The Beatrix Potter Society pp. 6, 7 (Rupert Potter); Getty Images pp. 4 (Express Newspapers), 8 (Rupert Potter/Time Life Pictures), 10 (Hulton Archive), 17 left (Andy Craword); Glow Images pp. 16, 23c (Westend61/Nabiha Dahhan); The Kobal Collection p. 21 (Weinstein Co); Newscom p. 19 (handout/KRT); Rex USA p. 11 (NILS JORGENSEN); Shutterstock pp. 12 (© wim claes), 13 (© mamahoohooba), 17 right, 23h (© Julie Boro), 23a (© Karel Gallas), 23b (© Petro Feketa), 23e (© Kevin Eaves), 23f (© Vasily Smirnov), 23g (© Falconia).

Cover photograph of Beatrix Potter pictured outside her Lake District house near Ambleside reproduced with permission of Getty Images (Popperfoto). Back cover image of a rabbit in meadow reproduced with permission of Shutterstock (wim claes).

Every effort has been made to contact copyright holders of material reproduced in this book. Any omissions will be rectified in subsequent printings if notice is given to the publisher.

Disclaimer
All the Internet addresses (URLs) given in this book were valid at the time of going to press. However, due to the dynamic nature of the Internet, some addresses may have changed, or sites may have changed or ceased to exist since publication. While the author and publisher regret any inconvenience this may cause readers, no responsibility for any such changes can be accepted by either the author or the publisher.

Contents

Some words are shown in bold, **like this**. You can find them in the glossary on page 23.

Who Was Beatrix Potter?

Beatrix Potter was a writer and **illustrator**.

She wrote and drew the pictures for children's books.

Beatrix Potter wrote many books that we still read today.

Her most famous book is *The Tale of Peter Rabbit*.

Where Did She Grow Up?

Beatrix Potter was born in 1866.

She grew up in London, England.

Beatrix had one brother, who went away to boarding school.

Like many girls at that time, she did not go to school.

What Did She Do Before She Was a Writer?

Beatrix loved painting when she was a child.

She had lots of pets and liked to draw and paint them.

She also liked to write in a **diary**.

She used a secret code so that nobody else could understand it.

How Did She Start Writing Books?

In 1893 Beatrix wrote a story in a letter to a sick boy.

She drew pictures for the story and called it *The Tale of Peter Rabbit*.

Beatrix decided to make the story into a book and **printed** 250 copies.

Then a company **published** the book and she became famous.

What Books Did She Write?

Beatrix wrote many other famous books.

She wrote several stories about rabbits, such as *The Tale of Benjamin Bunny*.

She also wrote *The Tale of Squirrel Nutkin* and *The Tale of Jemima Puddle-Duck*.

Children love to read about her funny animal **characters**.

What Did She Write About?

Beatrix bought a farm in the Lake District, in northwest England.

Many of her stories are set in the countryside around her farm.

Many people thought she didn't have a normal life for a woman at that time.

She often wrote about animals that didn't follow the rules, like her.

How Did Beatrix Draw the Pictures in Her Books?

Some of Beatrix's pictures are black and white.

She drew these pictures using pen and ink, like the artist in the photograph.

Other pictures in her books are in color.

She painted these pictures using paints called **watercolors**.

What Else Did She Like to Do?

Beatrix ran several farms in the Lake District, in England.

She raised animals, such as sheep, on her farms.

She looked after nature and animals all her life.

She also loved painting **landscapes** in the countryside.

Why Is She Famous Today?

People still buy Beatrix Potter's books today.

There are many Beatrix Potter gifts and toys.

There are museums and galleries on her life and work.

People have made movies about her life and her books, too.

Timeline of Beatrix Potter's Life and Work

1866	Beatrix Potter was born in London.
1893	She wrote *The Tale of Peter Rabbit.*
1901	She **published** *The Tale of Peter Rabbit.*
1905	She bought Hill Top Farm.
1913	She got married.
1930	Her last book, *The Tale of Little Pig Robinson,* was published.
1943	Beatrix Potter died.

Glossary

 **character** person or animal in a story

 **diary** book where someone writes down what they have done each day

 **illustrator** person who draws or paints pictures to go with a story

 **landscape** scenery

 **print** make many copies of something, for example a book

 **published** made into a book or put in a magazine and printed

 **watercolor** type of paint

Find Out More

Books

Some of Beatrix Potter's books: *The Tale of Peter Rabbit, The Tale of Squirrel Nutkin, The Tale of Jemima Puddle-Duck, The Tale of Benjamin Bunny, The Tale of Pigling Bland, The Tale of Mrs Tiggy-Winkle, The Tale of Two Bad Mice*, and *The Tale of Tom Kitten*.

Websites

http://www.hop-skip-jump.com/
Visit this website to find out more about Beatrix Potter and the World of Beatrix Potter attraction in the Lake District, in England.

Index